D1499878

DUTIES OF AN ENGLISH FOREIGN SECRETARY

Winner of the 2009 Fence Modern Poets Series
Selected by Martin Corless-Smith

Macgregor Card

FENCE BOOKS

*

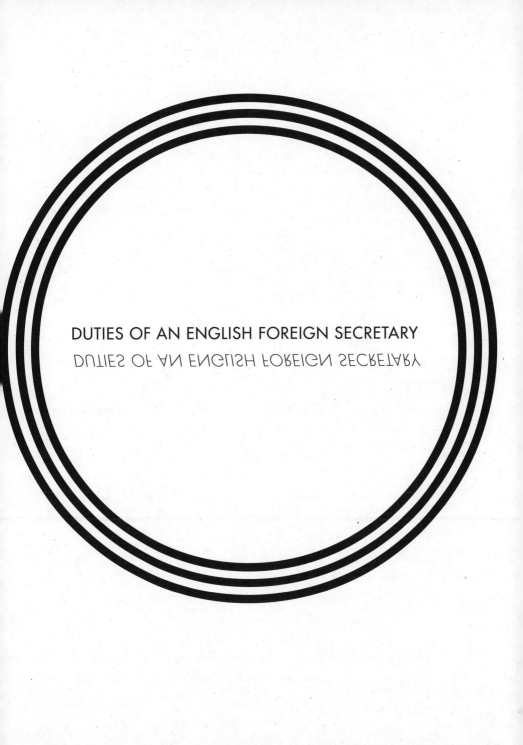

DUTIES OF AN ENGLISH FOREIGN SECRETARY

© 2009 by Macgregor Card
All rights reserved

Typeset in Dante and Futura

Cover photograph by Ellie Ga
Book design by Macgregor Card
Author acknowledgments appear in back

Published in the United States by Fence Books
Science Library 320
University at Albany
1400 Washington Avenue
Albany, NY 12222
www.fenceportal.com

Fence Books are distributed by
University Press of New England
www.upne.com

Fence Books are printed in Canada by
Westcan Printing Group
www.westcanpg.com

Library of Congress Cataloguing in Publication Data
Card, Macgregor [1974-]
Duties of an English Foreign Secretary /
Macgregor Card

Library of Congress Control Number: 2009932510
ISBN 978-1-934200-29-2

FIRST EDITION

CONTENTS

Oh the wold, the wold,
Oh the wold, the wold!
Oh the winter stark,
Oh the level dark,
On the wold, the wold, the wold!

Oh the wold, the wold,
Oh the wold, the wold!
Of the mystery
Of the blasted tree
On the wold, the wold, the wold!

—Sydney Dobell, "Wind"

POEM

There was a ship on fire last night.
I am ashamed and a burden to my friends.

CONTEMPT

(a cento of last words)

Now comes the mystery
I have no power
To move my arms
Applaud, my friends

I have no power
The comedy is over

Applaud, my friends
I haven't bored you
The comedy is over
And comedy is hard

I haven't bored you
Dante kills me
And comedy is hard
Repeat it to the golden floor

Dante kills me
Under the shade of the trees

Repeat it to the golden floor
I want you to undress me
Under the shade of the trees
Mozart! Mozart!

I want you to undress me
I knew it! I knew it!

Mozart! Mozart!
This is fidelity

I knew it! I knew it!
This is not Hamlet
This is fidelity
It's nothing, it's nothing

This is not Hamlet
Why do you weep
It's nothing, it's nothing
I borrowed a cock

Why do you weep
It was a mistake
I borrowed a cock
A king should die erect

It was a mistake
Leeches have red blood

A king should die erect
He has a story to tell

Leeches have red blood
—And you?
He has a story to tell
To wear my uniform

—And you?
I am not going

To wear my uniform
Keep me from the rats

I am not going
The gas is low

Keep me from the rats
For making enemies

The gas is low
More light
For making enemies
Stay for the sign

More light
In what peace can a Christian
Stay for the sign
Put out the light

In what peace can a Christian
Home in the dark
Put out the light
Eating its young

Home in the dark
Revolution is like Saturn

Eating its young
In the bloody ear

Revolution is like Saturn
Is the question
In the bloody ear
(The sign for NO)

Is the question
At Madison Square Garden
(The sign for NO)
Moose … Indian

At Madison Square Garden
Jefferson lives!

Moose … Indian
Empire, body and soul

Jefferson lives!
Goodnight
Empire, body and soul
I'm bored

Goodnight
I am surprised
I'm bored
Tell them I said anything

I am surprised
Fools who haven't said enough
Tell them I said anything

Now comes the mystery
Fools who haven't said enough
To move my arms

EMPHASIS MINE

> Along came a colossus, along came a colossus—
> but if I can't, but if I can't, but if I can't, but if I can't
> —Lorenzo Da Ponte, *Don Giovanni*

All this blank tape here
All of it mournful
Any can blow
   the long copper horn
   in love with oneself
   and so only blow
   as anyone—
not one relation
   to qualify
   everything
   that am called proud
a pure grammatical joke
   to salt the handshake
   and convert
   free salutation into policy

Put to mouth my true true
   ball and sing—

      I got my own / Lorenzo!
      mouth noises / Lorenzo!

I sing I got my own
   tenderness—

      Punitive early riser's / capital first step
      and experience of time

as incrementalized doubt
    Lorenzo! / CHORUS Lorenzo!

Put to mouth my due restraint
    Traitor in my applause crypt!

Bronze me twice / shame on me
    Traitor in / SOLO applause crypt!

If you put out the hand
  a little mince
Then put out your eye
  a little stick
If you put out the hand
  a little mince
Then put out your eye
    a little salt, but if I can't—
    a little mince, but if I can't—
  a little stick

SPASMODIC TRAGEDY
for Arlo Quint

Greet count and shoot
the tree's lights out
before it gets cold
it came to you remember
not the other way around
forget the right way down
sometimes
forget to go the right way down
born in the west
called Paris of the west
it was that nice
until the lights go out
to pieces
by command
it came to this
I promise
when they're on again
remember
count and reprimand

Say it's never over yet
crossed arms opening to memory
as fog shears
into thinning air
with prosecuting force
until that hopeful
goring sound
"forgot to catch your name"
that spectral heel
on my ear—
patternless left ear!

To jerk off all the lights
lose count in the dark
everywhere I shiver
moment's notice
ply one stranger
from its wind-eroded door
pleading through
and for the air
patternless wrong air
no sacrifice
goats tear the fog
a new one

Never heard the name
would have liked the west
or it's hard to say
what is their name
is a command—what name!
O air in air out
water out only home
O air out only
water out only store
O air in only
water in only flight
between the home and store
I came to you
in hope that lights need
screwing down a hall
beauty of a ladder on all fours
everywhere at once
how do I love to brace
your ladder down the hall
no saying—
hospitality in lighting store

LE SOLEIL ET LE POLICE DOG

Le soleil and le police dog
accept the offer of the road above
through the curtain of burning geese
I hope they will not catch fire
like the nudists do in Canada
or turn my eye to fat
hot coin for dark machine
to browse on the cave-money of suicide
wet rats dicking in the rain
heaven smiles on threat elimination
and the police-dog,
and the police-dog
smiles on me
I hope I will not catch fire
Le tellement croyable police dog
Le soleil et le police dog

POEM

Some day we're having
Some we're not as into
Some weren't fair
I claim I could say
it's nice in here ain't it
to *anyone*
I have my own reasons
I claim I could say it
to anyone

OFFICE OF THE INTERIOR

I hope the streetlamp will
show up tonight
in some disinterested way
once the tilted park has made it
out of view by law
Do you anticipate that it will rain?
Next volunteer
Just nod if you're
anticipating rain

What's the use of doing
little, please or nothing?
Laying tracks upon the quickly shaded chair
Maybe gone out or away, maybe there
The public are a few stone piers left off
in and out of shops and gardens
soon a railway crossing
drops the wooden board
almost in time
I'd like to visit anybody soon

NARY A SOUL
for David Gatten

Could if I could
Could if I no could

No, no could if I no could
Nary a soul

The light of day
The lamp of beauty

But the fire of sacrifice
I want to be

a colossus with an historian's pity
the ships to pass under me

silent / because / evacuated
It was the earliest it could ever be

in April
for just a moment

then—nothing
Nary a soul

Applause by hand
if joke by mouth

Three if by sea
One doesn't shape

what one pays for
One pays for

Sensual inaction is French
Argument German

The trade show, Protean
So visit the planets

Take yr mind off yr ego
At least

Be off the elegy
in time for Fontainebleau

If I could could could
No, could NO could could could

No, if I COULD could could could
If no no no no no NO no no no no no / NO no no no

If I could NO no no no NO no no no no no no no no
Nary a soul

All lighting paves
a choice of doors

for sense tellers
who want fast service

like Descartes in 1601
orange ribbon

fit to a cogitating wand
whose art of self-defense is pleasing

to the touch
it is unfair, he says

to humanize the blind
You can almost inter their fog

There are times
even glaciers must pass

on dry land
like the blind

There is no no
Or no no / no no

But no singular negation
Caspar David

Fucking Friedrich
that ice

looks cheap
get it out

of my shot
control your bodily eyesight

step onto your float
and wave wave wave wave

Out of nowhere, a wren
Out of luck, a shit

Poetry's no joke
But an endless and repetitive one

A German philosopher
in the American bush

Love is the sport of the numerous
barring the fulminous

Nobody looked alive
at the fire sale

Could if I could
No could if I no could

Nary a soul
If I could no

If I could no
If I could NO NO NO no no / could NO no no no no no no no no

No no no no no no no no no no
No no no no no no no no no no

Pricing is not physical exertion
as the steamer pulls

from tarry quay
met with holiday

swimmer on holiday
sand bar

I mean
auctioneer

was a jerk to my ship
two of my biscuits

completely got wet
I am only now

the beaten forward coin
of a journeyer

with no delivery
saying, quote,

buy a ticket
before the floodlights, sweeping, merge

The light of day
Nary a soul

The lamp of beauty
Nary a soul

The fire of sacrifice
If I could nary, nary, nary, nary, nary

It will be my last mistake
If I could nary, nary, nary, nary, nary, nary, nary

THE SLEEPING MONK OF INNISFALLEN

A shaking hand
give me nothing
watch it burn
I feel more
beautiful
than I am
Light cuts a shape
from the crowd
a shape that
for example
is not me
Sleep pounds
the sandstone
then
the sandstone
has some less
to go on
than before
or like
the poets say
a pretty girl
lives down the lane
or like
the Polish say
I live in Warsaw
and a pretty girl
lives down the lane
It's like I said
a traveller
has fallen asleep

inside my mouth
he was at war
in Pomerania
and Pomerania's
burnt out

POEM

The hours go few ways
too fast, how many fold
a shirt into their beast
I will not share it
for the world
it is more
than a handful
it is money
a vending song
too high for anyone to sing
except for money
Money will
sing the vending song
Too high for anyone to hear
except for money
Money will
hear the vending song
I cannot feel my face
I cannot feel my face
because I do not
get the joke
I am more
than a handful
I am money
I am Jack
the hierophant killer
and I must offer
to *pay* someone—
how many fold
a shirt into their beast?

How many fold?
I will not shore up
with the world
I need to spare
the will to sing—
Little bit hungry
yes so am I
Little bit hungry
yes so am I

POEM

Even spirits
have their
average signal
turned on you
simon tuesday
monday luke
goodnight
goodnight
in every way
you can imagine
fist on three
impress
the burning frost
pick up
where all these pistons
in the dove meat
left us
"all left riots"
welcome up
in arms
can't service
all these
middle-magic doves
just let go
like that
"next volunteer"
thanks all weather
psalm machine
thanks forever

POEM

You jacket! I said
I don't know what you want
but you can't afford *anything*, not even
cloud dividends

clouds were out filming
the firmament's collar of trees
where a parsonage beam fried through
but your horse threw you
and you hurt your face

A CHAIR IS NOT A SINGING MAN

for Eugene Ostashevsky

But the table is deaf
          like a metal rail
And flat as a board
          like the deaf
I know you hear this
          "beef needs salt"
But table understands
          "   "

Hands, where have they been
What are they like
Where do they creep and
Why do they succeed
Whose turn to grab
The emotional share of the bill
Who'll spring for the door
Extend your hand as a refrain

I went up my mountain now
     you go up yours
We circled the table now
     we are moved
We went around singing now
     you in your chair
Who can feel it is raining
     your hand in the choir

A friend is an event
that turns
on a covenant of

enduring speed
by the arm of debt
some table you can spin
with your two hands alone
for all your life
    it will not play a tune
as would a record
player needle

A hand is not a singing hand.
A chair is not a singing man.

THE RONDEL FRIENDSHIP

I be a lead male friend
I make you this beret of
pinecones to wear
at the hospital that helps the children with no hair
that are so hard to kill
in their silver tents
shirts passing over like birds of war
above the V of harvard rowers
barber music on their hot round balls
squealing in their jewelry box
a machine is only a device
a cardigan for pumping oars
depart heart, the vapor engine
sloshing in its cabinet of war
a device is only a conceit
for pressuring
an idea into consent, or a friend

And all legs, my escritoire
with faulty Charlotte Brontë software
I was taken on its first stair
pencil meats to gobble on all four
doors slamming in my silly wooden shoes
shirts passing over like birds of war
great athletes
with flaming cocktails
are hard to kill
off the cliffs of Dover
too hard to learn to live
to be incidental

when the pealing bells go off
there will be no time to retire
a friend is only a machine
delivering consent—
I be a lead male friend
in cabinet of war
there will be no time to retire
and there will be no time to retire

POEM

So full of longing, the day was mine warning
to sleep hard and never, the earth pied by trees
full of people, tradesmen, police and students
friendly from ear to glare. She was a beautiful
chauffeur who bent a horseshoe into wealth,
hand against my heart, now I sing a foolish song,
like a crossguard in a part of town, night came
and summer stuck it in smoke, I mean, tonight
I have work and I have memories, basically a ton.

POEM

I was often late, frequently lazy, not able
to tear a rent in space, though I won
a race, maybe two, I had nothing else to do
than instruct the dog to sleep and
fish to course the grey or turquoise deep.
Marie, there are bicycle tours cut short by
long and falling trees, bone-headed leaves
called off to war. I will not waste anymore.
They're waiting for me to die. I have no plans.
I have done nothing, been nothing, seen nothing.

I AM THE TEACHER OF ATHLETES

What is our penalty to be
                    like other folks alone
in a long string of pearls
worlds from california I believe
or the other coast they have
as if a ship of war
                    in a mariner's brochure
there is sport
in relation to parking
war in relation to song
everyone finish
            their seafaring poem?

I want all the drafts in american

        Most things are blue
            if you make them blue
        the most sorry dulcet
            the long way off lute
        the going down lark
            go down there lark
        wherever you are
            I'm pleased to be there
        har   har   har

                ★

There is no furniture for the impossible
This is only eternally true
The sun shines through the chief
The chief walks close to god

The lambs are ruining my favorite song
What do you think it sounds like
                              When you already know
What it sounds like

                    ⋆

A vast ocean weed
                 through a private garden
Bright corona
                 of the zero-responsibility corral

There are no organ donors on the riviera
There are no *slightly* effete british lords
There are no supernatural savings banks
There are sleeping and waking daughters
There are cars in south dakota
My car is an emissions caregiver
Put my car on the ground and back off
If you aren't gone by sundown
Love to the children
I hope they have not struck twelve
How painful it is to creep
Send them my sympathy
My disappointment and my flowers
The story is always the same
A skull appears inside your face
Then the applause breaks out
If I am the teacher of athletes
What is the meaning of wound?
What is the head in your hand?
Why is the ground on your face?

And I am
        the teacher of athletes
so do not
        insult the hooded beggar
and do not
        ambush the silver stag
with wrong
        correction officer's
enchanted staff
        so this is philadelphia
so make the kneeling
        swimmer's face I love

tsweeemuuuuuhrpfeeeeiiiitsss
        hwah   *hwah*   *hwah*
dah tsweeeeeemuuuhrpfeeeiiitsssss
        hwah   *hwah*   *hwah*
it is a kind of noise effect
                    to waste
clear admonitions on the bathing

Jupiter Saturn March
  Juvenal August Juvenal
Comedy Horace Choral
  Juno Juno Juvenal
Choral Javelin Farce
  Look no information
Quite so fine as oratory falls
  Over humiliated boys
Polishing a tyrant story shield

*

You should hear me play guitar on earth
  although
                        I got no recent tunes
I can't remember how to play
                              the old ones either
  not that I could stand them anymore
you should hear me play
                    guitar on earth some other time
      a long, long time ago

                *

Have I no poetry
                    as may promote
my learners' fury
                    or no vicious fork to stick
their vacant harp?

My heart has not
  a load-bearing wall
My horn
  no port of call
My lord
  it's getting dark

I want all the seas in american

Who do you think you are?
What are you going to do to me?
How are we going to get there?
Where are we going to go?

THAT OLD WOOLLY BLOODLETTING

In youth you tend to look rather frequently into a mirror,
not at all necessarily from vanity. You say to yourself,
"What an interesting face; I wonder what he'll be up to?"

—J. M. Barrie, "Courage"

Here is how pussycat /
I will show you to carry /
your unframed Cortez /
the conqueror portrait /
out of your nursery and into the forest
you'll kneel in to sleep
the cock of the walk
through falling of dead
unalterable leaves
you cannot yearn to ally
your friends with influence of law
Learn your Greek
You're a hero to open your book to learn
Jupiter failed as a nation
Though made by the giants

Australian is English!
I'd fold the universe
shut with tears
choking my prize
four crosses of shirts and trousers
in my fist
and a poor fellow's sword on my floor
Come *from* somewhere for a purpose
Go *to* somewhere for none

The angry burst   *into the room*
The mad burst   *into the wall*
as a victory poem
let it not be said
in the song that is so true
no ship moves up the one star night
without a plan to execute
in perpetuity, no no no no no no no
No, my boy, no no no no no no no no no no no
No no no, my boy, no no no no no no no no no no no no
The ship is a natural ship
as the wand is a natural wand
as the Englishman is hearing the frogs
uplifted as the queerest antique stag

Don't play with banker's straw, my boy
but talk the penny down
from its smoldering cloud
into your cup
you are that human shape
of public statuary
not to be
that town crier
in a meat locker
(armies travel on their stomachs)
Everyone's beloved
is a finite distance from your bed

Carry your portrait
    close to the vest
leave your liqueur
    set down by the fire
pick up the receiver

remember your Greek
and strum your important guitar.

You are doing what I tell you to do.
What more do you want us to do.
We will eat and then we will guard.
I want you to obey me willfully.
I do this to make us work.
The giants made me for this purpose.
We will guard and then we will sleep.
That is the action.
There'll be enough trouble.
I'm a hero to open your book.
We will work on the same shift.

RULE OF HOSPITALITY

> Come in quick, my happiness is at stake!
> —Pierre Klossowski

I alone were fraught with confidence
Doubt offset by counter-
Doubt to fuckdom come
But I need you
To *feel* my pretense
          A true friend cowers in my charity
And I in hers, alarmed hands
In each other's sopping open home

In one hound the rabbit fell hungry
And paced its affronted host
In the next hound a rabbit confused
The satiety of its hound
For its own, and both swagger
Beneath near star, ratified, cordial, aggrieved, retired

I alone were fraught with confidence
          The key in my hand
          Made me horny
Because I was telling the truth—
          I was here on my own authority
And it's none of my business
          Walking on air
With my friends to your door

GONE TO EARTH

I should have slept in a balloon
gone to Earth
hissing to own the sea
it is so difficult you dear
to be an underestimated resource
with the handshake of a coward
owned in thin air
I should have made an entry—

        Gone to Earth

                        No cowards

  Vast wall of bad clouds

               Tomorrow I will find some rain

No cowards

                 Night is kind of private

           Someone lost a bad shoe

    It is too far away

             Don't see any cowards today

I can tell it's difficult to stay clear
from lovers who try
to be in my song, why don't they try
is one example, why not try
      maybe they can tell I should
have made an entry—

             There's a man-made coin

    I feel cocked over

                So much glare

      I speared a burning ant

                                out of courtesy
        by the way
                                what are cockchafers
            in *Systema Naturae*
        by Carolus Linnaeus
                        Can't be Latin—Gone to Earth

Feel stalling wind / Fear small erotomachiad
Don't know how to breed today
So many lose it on the beach
They made a bad horn follow some glare
    and ran a fox onto your property
but village fox don't run
    your property or run the dash
onto your collar into court
    but everywhere you turn
a circumprecious juror says it
    my what dashing mantles
to parade in wooden cordoned acre
    a seething in a field of weed abatement

clean dogs   drama   line of clean sight
no   clay in the face   big star
the robe that leaves me hanging

hold the coward's handshake long
as in a thriving doubles hammock
just a clasp   is the duration of his treaty

If we're darling in the air you'll know me
    by contract as long as you hold me
and I by yours as long as you, dear, me

and snitching the night away
reporters on a wire, snitching! snitching!
   snitching the night away
I want us to feel our best in front
   of the summery judge
and pretty good to meet you
   blowing off steam
weeping to the courthouse to grow old
   ready to be unhandsome
in a likeable odd coat
   in the weeds with a beast or two
                              to prove we beat
To bed or be the creeps

How moody can I get in flight
Should have made an entry
Should have seen a beast
Flying over dashing rocks! but cannot hear

                              flashing horns!

Beasts, none
Clouds, huh

        I'm sure I noticed someone make

                              a bad deal
                        in the weeds
        Tomorrow I will shoe

                        my favorite leg

                              points down
            Often feeling talked about

                        or bored
I'll start to count, but it will pass

                  Haven't seen one beast today

Gone to Earth

It is too near—maybe I can tell
It's difficult to clear the air

Tomorrow I will find a kind of private night

TO FRIEND-TREE OF COUNTED DAYS

> A hurricane is stripping the woods
> A key will be my dwelling
> The feint of a fire the heart confirms
> And the air whose capture seized it
>
> —René Char, "Effacement du peuplier"

I am climbing a tree
too high for words
whose leaves are as green
as they ought to be
the only shade at night
that meets me is my own
Johnny Élan forever
I hate to confess
sometimes I feel
volunteered upon
by a formal quality of sky
cowed trust
in movement and volition
put to love
propensity itself to feel
a little black mandate
yes, for consent
and resignation

white cloud
            black cloud
white goose
            deaf goose

I wish I was not
on a burning tree
but a tree that was
really on fire
though the emphasis
is my own
it is anyone's place
to be here, the view
I can only imagine
is probably astounding
if seen in generous light
though consolation
is that debt of love knows
infinite regress
I thought was said
that debt of love
knows infinite egress
and so the pines
are bright
because they are all
around me

white cloud
                 black wood
white cliff
                 black wreath

Johnny Élan was here
his knife as fast
as it ought to be
the tree he seized
grew high

the tree I sing
you know that way
it is the shade
that meets you
is your own
like any other feeling
spent apart
from green hard home
below red star
to shrill formality
one thing
I do not lack the sense in
to expire

How long is the comedy
                    about me?

How far to the barrier
                    I know?

What is there to sing
                    but a round?

What is there to seize
                    but a while?

What is there to counter
                    but fall?

THE LIBERTINE'S PUNISHMENT

I was grabbed by the arm near the stairwell
Then grabbed by the arm near the door
Next grabbed by the arm near the forest
Until grabbed by the arm near a dark
                  embankment of ferns—
They are drenched and they are on fire
They are only orange lights in the steam
Motioning down to the sea
Something is moving beside me
Nothing's supposed to be there
Either I have a heart of stone
or I haven't got a heart
perhaps I only have a stone
and that stone is *not* my heart
and that stone is neither *like* my heart
for I have no heart, I only have a stone
following down to the sea

                  Things as they are
vanish not to ask questions
in the interval some friend departs, another
red photographed birthday
lost at low lighting
                oral exam for the genius
who builds the first fog machine
not also having a horn machine
                  Incredible, yet
the true cloud's anvil
seats just the one songbird doing its taxes
purple, nothing personal

              Things vanish not as they are
but as they were to be remembered

hard to bathe them in the cold
low lighting on their crumpled doors of oak
Young legs in a restrained
starburst pattern do appear
and do not light the way
they are drenched
and they are on fire
they are only
orange lights in the steam
motioning down to the sea
Something is moving beside me
Nothing's supposed to be there

I was grabbed by the arm near the highway
Then grabbed by the arm near the shore
Until grabbed by the leg near the stone
                       at the ocean's floor

THE MERMAN'S GIFT
for Karen Weiser

Brother I need back my sticks
I hope you make it forward

Hope you learn to range
by grass depressed by possibility alone

One and every
actionable blade of glamor

in a ranger's vatic underfauna
If we go there

I'm a total wreck my brother
carried off at totalcy

I need for you to wreck
upon yourself

the salvage you recover
from me

and I love you
I need back the sticks I loaned you

How else will I say I be
the sun's own paned adjudicant

to the peal of shade rotation
around every quitter's cone

if you can't turn
the simple wrecking lamp on me

Remember anyone at all
who doesn't know you is a quitter

and anything that doesn't act upon you
is a quitter

almost any people, glass or metal
any mountain you could think to name

has quit beneath a quitter's vegetation
not to mention

all those quitter leaves so many you would think
they never had a chance

almost any
furniture and window overlooking

every city's quitter signal—
wish you'd come inside from their neglect

if it were even possible
to sit here with me in the broadest public

lost at sea, a bench in memory of strangers
placed through everybody's moving rain

(pretend you could endure
a friend's wide-open shower scene)

as if half-surf wherever
stranded as a cave-mouth weed

there'd be a time
to say my brother is survived by our merbrother

"Take care"
"Take care forever, no!"

Proverb not
you are your friend's own family

but you are your friend's own family
robinson

"Meet me in my chambers"
better "Meet me in my brother's chambers"

Hit me in the folk
I am so high on you

When you weren't succeeding
anywhere

not even by your standard
have my sticks I said

I hope they bring us closer now
they have to be returned

Just think of it as obligation
without flooring hesitation

(pretend you're not ashamed
to dance in public)

I just want an understanding
that exceeds

without excluding unremitting favor
or favors accountability

over accessory to
(any single) fraud

I hope you make it forward
I need back the sticks

Ever see a merman put away
its roaming horn in tears

because you gave it all
no signal?

Hope you never do
on my account

I hope you honor all your debts
I'm so in love with you

WIND

The wind comes after the leaves and takes them on trips all over the world. Sometimes there is only one last leaf and it is sad, because it thinks it has been forgotten. But the wind comes back for that lonely leaf and takes it along the most wonderful trip. The lonely leaf is blown around the world and sees all the wonderful things that are possible to see. Then it comes back to my yard because it misses me. It settles beneath the tree and waits. It is tired and worn from its long trip. I think it wanted to return because it hadn't met anyone in all the world it liked as much as it liked me. I keep that leaf. It is very old, but I keep that leaf.

POEM

I could burn these trees all day
They are worthless and fallen behind
My father is a beautiful animal
in poor form, you see, a little straw
keeps the chill of the earth from his body
I was never one to get my hand
to cool in smoke, he says
A remnant of snow
is like a pennant you can wave
from your ditch, he says
So long as I am there with you
nothing hard can fall on you
How can failure start and failure end?
Failure is failure, it is a riot.
Just lower your head, the flames spread, he says.

THE LIBERTINES' ANNOUNCEMENT

Today the mayor planted
    oranges symbolizing rage
Tomorrow, oranges
    symbolizing hope
A third day, oranges
    standing in for rage
    as well as hope
will soon revert to rage
    and the tree
is nowhere to be found

                    AT ONCE
Divert all steam ships
Make for silent
                    golden film's
maritime farewell scenes
least   it feels that way to flood
            these broken ribbons

into sunlight
concrete
busting sunlight

air-dropped from, wherever,
the stars, in a language
you can understand
to warn you of invasions
you can understand from afar
            or from a field reporter
radioing presence to the trees

municipal and goldenrod the trees
that we were tenants
earning blaring living
wages governed by
those often human agencies

as bent afloat
a literal
bottomless stream

Did you hear the one
  about the Straits of Magellan?
No—listen—I'm asking you
  if you heard the one
about the Straits of Magellan
  not telling you

        Could if I could, could if I no could
        No, no could if I no could

Can't make out
            whose yellow duty light goes on
Couldn't they be made
            to seem to all agree
as public road and tunnel lamps at dusk
            or televion news
ALL DAY cannot make out
            the field reporter's uniform
            for (upward mobile) uniform
of archaeologists
            share light-emitting lunch
for extra money comb
                the sand for ordinance

                    when dressed
for diplomatic travel—
          puffy German peasant blouse

                        DID YOU HEAR
All libertines announce
All trains stop in the Antipodes
this time of year
THIS IS NOT THE CITY
              of the blessèd call center worker
A stranger cannot
          make a living as a memoir
We cover more ground in the hero
In fact we get in a car and go
Emotion one / emotion two / emotion three
Etcetera, except with feeling and
                          an ox named Babe

    Could if I could
          Could if I no could
              No, no could if I no could

Today the mayor planted
    oranges symbolizing rage
Tomorrow, oranges
    symbolizing hope
Later, stands of oranges
    symbolizing rage
as well as hope
    revert to rage
and the trees
              nowhere to be found

POEM

London, it is very ornery
Heathrow Airport, it is a nudist colony

DUTIES OF AN ENGLISH FOREIGN SECRETARY

Moon, refrigerate the weeping child
and guard his frozen brook
There is no thing between the woods
like music of the band
and I've got friends in London, no I've
got *friends* in *London*
lawyer in their hearth or billion starry heath
in the language of mine
that they laugh at
delphiniums rev up the fire
really look at them go
take into the throat
a snowfield gas
a Crimean slogan
In England
or in sum
no papers go off bang to pad the fog

My nation bears repeating and adores
the hermit maudit rising without name into gorgeous claimant lumber
Here's your forest
visitor—soft psssst of the oar—
will you hear a bird parlando
necking at your door
That duck will float
should it be born
my face from off its neck is torn
I owe so much, I have no thing
the rest I'll leave the poor
I've seen the truth, I have my mind

I *have* to have that telephone
it fit in the hand
a hundred times over
and that's not all
that's everything
Compare this to the British Isles
what I cannot describe
what I saw—
Prospero wailed on Ariel
and Ariel wailed
"What a boom year for material!"
By the way
all this takes place
on my lawn
it has nothing to do with love
it is perfunctory
it is the end of the year
it is your idea and I want more of it
Wrap my bonny hood in every paper
on the rack and please to have
a horse to cart
the grocery off my back
Now it's got late and I will go and will be back

In the forest some hear winds adjust
a funny tuft of seed
Where is that song or stiffly-collared child
beating on a pot, but in the forest I do not
I only hear my friends are sawing in the fog
Some hear their mouth in front
of that but face perform
the words "light company at four"

and a "mall to leaf through eye-correction
literature at eight" and couldn't that be great
I'd even trade it for a song and some hear beasts
perform an even-tempered chorus
I only hear those friends
are sawing in the fog

I found myself in a wood of chairs
The birds were thin as wires
When information fails, light falls
The office clock to airy thinness beat
Is it not gold to have been cheek
in front of that but guilt to bear
Take that, I live the life for the dog you eat
Youth to fortune
instrument you are prohibitive
I want to walk a line
I want to play my dove
in a magic show about John Donne
but everybody does
but everybody does
steal all the gold and silver
fall down stabbed, light a pity candle
then get up again and quote
I go to sleep and then get up again

Moon, refrigerate the sitting child
and guard his frozen brook
There is no thing between the woods
like music of the band
and I've got friends in London, no I've
got *friends* in *London*

None of my friends reads poesie
All around them was trees
These friends called me sir
I have said things I would love
to have been true, but thought
and act are crammed with chairs
Soft visitor sit down, and then?

POEM

I lift my eyes to the visible tree,
not easy, in view of its quiet leaves
They are showy mirrors
and the morning is without wind

YIELD TO TOTAL ELATION

It's beginning to rain and go silent

If you've got a fern to comb through
now's the time

Soon everything are windows
in decline

Stars are practically a floor-sale
and recitation, speech

Outside the cars are bored
beyond their years
so are we

So were they angels basically
all brains and apprehension
patterned as a jeweller's window
in the standing water
or was it just
a streetlamp you know
casting aspersions

O move along, move along friend
There's nothing to see
Don't stand there and try
and *not* see anything either, it's nothing
and it's not in the mood to be seen
Move along
Nothing is too big and too small
To move along

STUDIES OF SENSATION AND EVENT

for Chris Martin

I don't feel like doing anything
So I won't do or feel like doing anything
I won't move or hold still, speak, not speak, marry, not marry, go it alone
I'd regret trying anything impossible
I won't do anything I'll regret
And I don't feel like doing anything at all
So I won't do anything or feel like doing anything impossible
I won't move or hold still (impossible)
I won't feel like moving or holding still
I mean
This is all to say
I can't dance
What's more, I am a creep
I feel like a creep
I regret that I am a creep
It is impossible not to regret feeling like a creep
If only I had learned earlier to not feel like doing anything
To not do anything or feel like doing anything I'd regret
To not regret doing anything or regret feeling like doing anything impossible
Then I would not be a creep
I would have no regrets
I would have no impossible feelings
"No Dancing"

TOGETHER WE SHALL WIN
THE TITLE OF BLUEBEARD

I've already seen you
And I already know
Everything there is
To know about you
That violin!   Put down
That violin and hear
The thunder of my cowardice

My thunder and my cowardice
I swear upon this hand
That if you find
Some girl along the way
Try and bring her with you too!
I'll take upon myself
To amuse us
Until it is the time
To console us
For my sorrow
and her cruelty

But listen and have mercy—
It's entirely her fault
Not mercy upon her, then,
Mercy upon me, then,
Already you have heard
That it's entirely her fault
That she's learned
Everything I didn't need
To have another learn
Enough to tremble

I'll avenge her wrongs
I mean, the things she
Brought upon me
I'll avenge upon myself
To console myself
From myself
And dry my awful lashes
On her hand
But if you find
Some girl along the way
Bring her with you too!

My love is an aversion
Eligible for taxation—
Seventy I have loved
In the northern city
Ten years of affliction
Is not enough, I thought
To myself, for the seventy—
Eighty you have loved
Eighty in the eastern city
Not even enough
You thought to yourself
For my seventy—my friends
Have loved my own seventy!
What for my friends
Who loved my own
Seventy, then, what, then!

I've already seen you and
I already know
Everything there is to know
About that violin!

Put down that violin and ice
Your exhausted proboscis

You're dead if you move
To block the liar's boar
From charging at my breast
Protector of veals, my breast
Repeats the ancient song
To kill a tiger, throw it to the dogs
To kill a tiger, throw it, throw it!
Such a marvel it will be!
Use up the fraud
You save for laughter
Throw it to the dogs!

I want to think I'm dying
In every direction
I want to depart
Through every possible door
Look out if you touch me
And wait for my blows
A storm is gathering my effects
You're dead if you move
To block the liar's boar
From my shooting coward's arrow
Friend, what is an animal, friend,
But a cubit to measure my groin

The kindness you could show me
Could move me
To persecute me, a libertine
With his beard of friends
I'll swear it by this hand

My autoharp I'll play to ruins
And surrender you
My friends, this hand and throat
My prize, this sword of relatives
That long, my wealth and lovers
A catalogue of broken faith

A faithful love must yield
Put down the violin
And with this harp invite
The stone colossus in
To dine, not arbitrate but judge
And with this breath
Protector of thieves
Command to him from memory
This catalogue of broken faith—
My friends, their lovers' hands
My prize, this fraud, your faith, my life
You're dead if you move
My bust of Mercury
No marvel it will be

Your own colossus I'll invite
To you, you, libertine
With your beard of friends
You and you and you and you
Speak loudly and stay
Speak loudly to us and stay with us
To see us on our way
To nothing, together
We shall win the title of Bluebeard
It is ours already
Already you have heard
We win the title of Bluebeard

PETRARCH, LAURA, DE SADE AND GOD

Elective Affinities is a novel by Goethe. In it, he affirms the plausibility of platonic love, cautioning that it requires each lover have a satisfactory and undivorcible spouse. "Four persons are required to work the miracle." Two persons and two persons deceived. Two lovers locked in the non-embrace of feigned physical aversion deceive two spouses through the artifice of physical affection. Sustained aversion with the lover is the purpose. Sustained affection with the spouse is the means. Goethe was not writing of Laura and Petrarch, but consider. Laura's person deceived is her husband, Hugh de Sade. A clergyman, Petrarch's lover deceived is God. God is the fourth person required to work the miracle. He is deceived to sustain the non-embrace of Petrarch and Laura. Imagine, "You must not speak to me" she whispers to Petrarch in passing. "You must always speak to me," he then whispers to God.

PANTOUM

I believe without a doubt
Christians have a right to shout
I believe without a doubt
Christians have a right to shout

Christians have a right to shout
Christians have a right to shout
I believe without a doubt
I believe without a doubt

HEY FRIEND

for Brandon Downing

Hey friend, as you cross the street I notice—no reward from heaven plays whist into all I have lost.

I'm sorry to hear—can't talk—tears don't make the beans grow, Christian.

As you turn from me I notice—I can't sleep at night and toss like a vacation screw, except I'm quite alone! My Christian name is debt consolidation.

Then economize on fire, with them unshakable candles. And it'd be better if you asked for money without awful letdown.

I'll move to buy a few sticks on a contingent bill of sale, with four-weeks' right of cancellation. Good-bye! I'll miss your straight bangs and council face.

*

Hey friend, you're like a god covered in skin. Visit my counter! It takes alms to beg alms.

Skin, that's where they found my former sadness, hair. And you, you think that you're a clerk?

I know that I'm a clerk. Six thousand are known to flower in the great family of departmental flora. It's the season for allowing fresh, sharp flowers again and again to *pay* for the breeze. Some day I will make sure they do, some day I'll *know* I am a manager.

Well, friend clerk, your muzzle's in a rich clump of blooms. Leave it there a while, I'm going away, truly.

Then my heart's in the grip. I'm in debt. An old boarder passing through, napping and carrying on. A friend says to a corpse, "I can say *anything* to you, and you can understand."

★

Hey friend, you took part in my arrest—they took me from the forest and put me to good use.

I'm sorry, friend. You have to remember I'm a veteran of unrehearsed period-poetry of terror. I love you like a father his brother, but need *burly inland revenue*, fast.

So you bounce my head like a horse language / tap / tap tap / tap tap tap. What is it to be a friend in destitute times?

Poor friend, I am so fond of you, and now *you* now it, so take notice—I am about to show that you can *never* have seen me, anywhere.

POEM

This oceanliner's overrun with fathers
telling me how to skin a weasel

Easier said than done when someone's
put the dogface on your buddy

POEM

Once a liar, always a judge
Once a liar, always a judge

THE GIANT AND THE HUNCHBACK

Horsey, Horsey, I too am aware /
You wouldn't terribly mind /
On your way into town

Brother and sister—*Piatto!*
Where do you cool
Your bonne amitié?
Where is bonne amitié larder?

            Brother face
And its lone pneumatic tear

            Sister face
And its butch throbbing shiner

            Grope for the water
Parting it badly, trying it out

            Right there in our face
How to respect

            That fuck-ecology
Of an upturned thumb
And its crude nativity-bush
In full calf, what do they
            Model to play
Sisters and brothers—*Piatto!*
When all a neighbor cannot
Fuck to save its spaniels' lives
            Where do you stage
Your bonhomie, where is
(Your own) Macbeth horse-opera

Counting its age in hoof-beats
On a floor of dead cocks

Friends, it is the distant *Fremder*
Paying for the love of neighbor

As so you course / My knee through town
It is the distant fiend
Supplies my leg your groin with feeling

If only we could see
The distance commerce
Of the snow that paces home
Snowy horned latinate delegate in horrible (own) doorframe
Danger, *mes enfants,* giant!
Danger, *giants,* shaft!

OUTSIDE the owl inseminates
A gorgeous mylar balloon

If only we could see ourselves
Right there in the face
Without touching ourselves
Like pictures keeping still
Or go to town
As pictures mailed to relatives
That keep in touch

Thrashing we'll reserve
As a conservation measure
For a second night together
Horsey, Horsey, I too am aware
But I turn off here—

Piatto! Goodnight!

POEM

I almost built
a house
for a dog
do not intrude
upon its
shut and used
revolting
door

do not
attend

let none of
your
feeling ennoble
a witness

but who will
stoop
to mate
me

POEM

For recreation I put on
the small volcano
a song about the one
who got away
The sun comes out
with every feather
where it ought to be
but one of us was dead
in every note they sang
to beat the hummingbirds
You're sometimes bright
though between
you and me
you don't have any
food, you said
Came their reply
There are some
BLOODY BUNS
in the cake tin

FAREWELL PARABLE

I know a bird in Maryland
that got away with everything
including murder and obesity
It wouldn't move nor say a word
The blood that left its face
could not return
                    One should travel
when one is young, it said
I did, you should have
seen me then, it said

MY DONKEY, MY DEAR
for Olivier Brossard and Claire Guillot

My donkey, my dear
Had a pain in his head
A kind Russian lady gave him
A bonnet of red
And little shoes of lavender
Lav—lav—lavender
And little shoes of lavender
To keep him from the cold

My donkey, my dear
Had a pain in his throat
Your donkey, my dear
Had a pain in his hand

A pain in his head
A pain in his throat
A bonnet of red
A button-up coat
A pain in his hand
Mittens lying around
And little shoes of lavender
Lav—lav—lavender
And little shoes of lavender
To keep him from the cold

URSUS MEMENTO MORI

	The bears are too much to suffer
and so	I forget to say things to animals.
	I can denigrate bear without language.
	Its judicial impartiality
will not upstage	my expansionist hospitality.
	Its philosophy is vulnerable to physique
	and mechanical action.
	The power of bear knowledge
intolerable	because unvexed by mental concourse.
	The bear does not speak against the sun.

	Come vary my iron plate
bear.	Stand a little closer to me
bear.	Now a little further
bear.	Elevate upon my friends
	the shaft of the hand, sailor.
	Some sports they are not
	arena sports, philosopher.
	We cannot see the bear
	as the bear sees
luminous spheres	where our heads might have been.
	Everywhere. A hole in the ground.
Two shovels.	One rake.
	Nothing fascinates the plants.
Don't you wish	the dead could feel the rain in your face.

No man is a hero to his valet.
Heroes cannot smell their lovers.
The bear is some valet to man.

                    Then, a man who loves some bear
can also   be said to smell some bear.
                    Everything comes to rest
                    at knowledge through stupefaction
but how   to stop the magician
                    from touching the ladies
                    Nature reduced to extension
                    I can hardly suppress my gorge
                    Ad astra per aspera, ursi
                    non numero nisi serenas.
                    To the stars, through hardship
                    I only mark the hours of the day.

OVERHEARD IN THE BATHYSPHERE

Each public hammer's minute's work
there is the fact you hope
memory does not force the past to happen
                out of my cold dead hands
as seconds pass, what do you not
through striving say
                "You are too late"

"I need to show you in private"
           a pervert's hand-elevator
        to bare stars
like stars in hesitation
            all kinds of bodies agrees
to dread error, the nagging dove
this whole soft eye of a deer
              who can find
the robin in the venison
           who sees it there

Of course it's like a song, the song
Who can find the robin / in the venison who sees it there
peeping / out of shot
somewhere just itinerant enough
Actionable wrong ear
Delay, I thought you said a man field

I thought you said you were in danger
            to the lenient decay of private song
           forced by memory

to have been sung
                        without alternative
There is an art of flying why not
there is an art to sinking
                        and it is the arc of song

Who moves to hold
                        a dancer's leap
                        an observation tower
at cross-bathos
        with applauding audience
                        be asleep
on calculably public chairs
to each their nebulous own house
if the image of a rider's head
                        do we do this nebula favors not
                        this one? *this* house? .

House rules forbid dead relatives
like the wedding moth
                        its lost blank cape
When I'm inside reminds
"you are too late"
                        to act alone
house doors play badly in a storm
to willing residents
                        recollects

municipal axe

SHIPFILM

for Stephanie Barber

I hope the curtain will not touch me
It would be my last mistake

I have been through water
I don't work beyond the water—

The sun moves across the water
And I like to see the ground I'm walking on

So I follow where it goes
And let them see me where I wander

There might be friends along a shore
I will not know unless I follow

There might be friends below the water
Moving toward the other shore

I need to see where they are moving
And why they hurry from me

Each day from land to water
I won't know unless I follow

I will follow through the water
I will let the curtain touch me

If I let the curtain soak
They will see into my home

It will be my last mistake
There are so many people

Who I do not know
So many people

I repeat myself
I do not know

FEAR AND TREMBLING AND
THE SICKNESS UNTO DEATH

People commonly refrain
They sleep in windy acres
Afraid of speaking plainly
They commonly go down
It's okay to be intelligent
It's free to be a towering wall of bounty
(it's understood to be beautiful)

People mounted on a stairs
or on a ladder in a savings bank
speak humanely with assurance
to the knight of faith
Their hearts are in receivership
Each human to its oily violet shed
So join me in my scarlet modest house
In the playroom it's so cold today
For I am ready　　　Yes you may

Although a hammer is not sick for hope
Hard mirrors end incredibly
(the windows of a lighting store)
We'll take our cart down to the store
No one is there in the store at night
We'll pick up some things we *need* in the store
But we won't stay long in the store at night

Although a hammer is not sick for faith
Why did Abraham do it
in the story of Abraham

and yet they *extol* Abraham?
I cannot love like Abraham
Faith is not *sort of* aesthetic
short of ideas like the story of Abraham
I'd care for a puppet to frighten Abraham
A story puppet with a flaming sword

I can endure no longer to remain
(upon a doorstep in the rain)
Although dark nights reward a street
with famous snow-swept breweries
the meat upon my table has no heart
So join me in my scarlet modest house
In the playroom it's so cold today
My heart is called a snow-swept meat

        For I am ready   Yes, you may

     For I am ready   Yes, you may

          For I am ready   Yes, you may

     For I am ready   Yes, you may

AFTERNOON OF A FOREIGNER

O faun / in sensitive pants / run out of your tune
I fear in your loin / too distant a heat
The sun = size of a *human* foot
You ought to learn English and carry a gun
The world is not your former tavern lawn
You may not enter to talk for the night
You may not enter to talk

                          or enter to rest
You may not enter to talk for the night
If you know something to hear
about weeping

              hear it
or someone might tear down your eyes

           ★

When the church was young
        with whaling tours installed
into a theater of well-lit rain
as if that Roman were about to
      Hail / Farewell   *Hail / Farewell*
material hands that divide and rule
a violent resource of red mist
made for filing through

Sweet clerical book in the lilac bush
you ought to learn English
and carry a gun
you are partially ugly
as a wild bird

that people do not like
in the Bank of England

      unending mass of spilling leaves
from penurious bending willow
fall to a choir in maybe a chapel
maybe a corvette
maybe a chapel
painted red meat

     is *inside* the nut
until shot in the field
and sprayed

     through a window of glare
free to the air for some to hear
where the world lay open, yes
to a sermon's matching hemisphere

    ★

I would like to say
it would have been kind
to tell you sooner
there is no word
that is always false
in a kind of black frame
like hands to the harp-shaped lake
go pale metal ambulant fish
that cannot be allowed
to pray for rain
The sea is wide! intones

      the heaven is high

the ghost leaves home
for a whaling career it says
to a flashing / empty / chair

this is how you disappear
endorse each room
with a metal word of kindness, *ping*
                   like a business check

This is the King James version of this poem
        a little sad music to wind the clock
you may not enter to talk for the night

This is the little sad music of this poem
You may not enter to rest

POEM

A boy lifting a foreign whistle
most things
wheel me across the lawn
I too would drop the brightest wallet
of ideas to hold little
but mighty sea, lord of plenty amused
without skill or purpose
any folk player in the dark park
Bright kill, for all its fleece /
a tiger is not bestial in the least /
it could not be much later /
in the year

NOTES / SOURCES

This book is a companion volume to Karen Weiser's *To Light Out* (NY: Ugly Duckling Presse, 2010). Most poems have several lines or phrases in common, drawn from weekly collaborations, 2001-2008.

"Ursus Memento Mori" was commissioned by Karl Krause for "Earth on Stone on Earth Is Naturally So", an earthworks project and installation at Flashpoint Gallery. It was composed while buried to the neck with four poets in the Nethermead zone of Prospect Park (Brooklyn).

"Duties of an English Foreign Secretary" is the title of an 1852 essay by the Spasmodic poet, Sydney Dobell, collected in *Life and Letters of Sydney Dobell* (London: Smith, Elder & Co., 1878).

"Together We Shall Win the Title of Bluebeard" takes language from Lorenzo Da Ponte's *Don Giovanni*.

"Wind" and "I lift my eyes to the visible tree" are adaptations of found (though since lost) poems.

"My Donkey, My Dear" is based on a French nursery rhyme.

ACKNOWLEDGMENTS

The author would like to thank the editors of the following publications, where poems first appeared: *Arsenal, Baltimore Is Reads, Best American Poetry 2007, Brooklyn Rail, Can We Have Our Ball Back?, Fell Swoop, Fence, Ink Node, KGB Bar Lit, Lungfull!, Puppyflowers, The Recluse, Whitman Hom(m) age* and *Woodland Pattern.*

Special thanks to Martin Corless-Smith, Rebecca Wolff, Colie Collen, Eugene Ostashevsky, Brandon Downing, Albert Mobilio, Ellie Ga, Chris Martin, Kendra Sullivan, Megan Ewing, Olivier Brossard, Claire Guillot, Arlo Quint, Stacey Szymaszek, Karl Krause, Lynn Xu, Josh Edwards, Heather McHugh, Erin McMonagle, David Adamo, Zoe Ward, Martha Westwater, Peter Gizzi, Elizabeth Willis, Michelle Levy, Keith and Rosmarie Waldrop, Ma, Pa, Brother Zac and Sister Karen.

Cover photos courtesy of Ellie Ga and Taraexpeditions.org.

Fence Books is an extension of *Fence*, a biannual journal of poetry, fiction, art, and criticism that has a mission to redefine the terms of accessibility by publishing challenging writing distinguished by idio-syncrasy and intelligence rather than by allegiance with camps, schools, or cliques. It is part of our press's mission to support writers who might otherwise have difficulty being recognized because their work doesn't answer to either the mainstream or to recognizable modes of experimentation.

The Motherwell Prize is an annual series that offers publication of a first or second book of poems by a woman, as well as a one thousand dollar cash prize.

Our second prize series is the Fence Modern Poets Series. This contest is open to poets of any gender and at any stage of career, and offers a one thousand dollar cash prize in addition to book publication.

For more information about either prize, visit www.fence portal.org, or send an SASE to: Fence Books/[Name of Prize], New Library 320, University at Albany, 1400 Washington Avenue, Albany, NY, 12222.

For more about *Fence*, visit www.fenceportal.org.

FENCE BOOKS

THE MOTHERWELL PRIZE

Aim Straight at the Fountain and Press Vaporize	Elizabeth Marie Young
Unspoiled Air	Kaisa Ullsvik Miller

THE ALBERTA PRIZE

The Cow	Ariana Reines
Practice, Restraint	Laura Sims
A Magic Book	Sasha Steensen
Sky Girl	Rosemary Griggs
The Real Moon of Poetry and Other Poems	Tina Brown Celona
Zirconia	Chelsey Minnis

FENCE MODERN POETS SERIES

Duties of an English Foreign Secretary	Macgregor Card
Star in the Eye	James Shea
Structure of the Embryonic Rat Brain	Christopher Janke
The Stupefying Flashbulbs	Daniel Brenner
Povel	Geraldine Kim
The Opening Question	Prageeta Sharma
Apprehend	Elizabeth Robinson
The Red Bird	Joyelle McSweeney

NATIONAL POETS SERIES

The Black Automaton	Douglas Kearney
Collapsible Poetics Theater	Rodrigo Toscano

ANTHOLOGIES & CRITICAL WORKS

Not for Mothers Only: Contemporary Poets on Child-Getting & Child-Rearing — Catherine Wagner & Rebecca Wolff, editors

A Best of Fence: The First Nine Years, Volumes 1 & 2 — Rebecca Wolf & *Fence* Editors, editors

POETRY

Stranger — Laura Sims
The Method — Sasha Steensen
The Orphan & Its Relations — Elizabeth Robinson
Site Acquisition — Brian Young
Rogue Hemlocks — Carl Martin
19 Names for Our Band — Jibade-Khalil Huffman
Infamous Landscapes — Prageeta Sharma
Bad Bad — Chelsey Minnis
Snip Snip! — Tina Brown Celona
Yes, Master — Michael Earl Craig
Swallows — Martin Corless-Smith
Folding Ruler Star — Aaron Kunin
The Commandrine & Other Poems — Joyelle McSweeney
Macular Hole — Catherine Wagner
Nota — Martin Corless-Smith
Father of Noise — Anthony McCann
Can You Relax in My House — Michael Earl Craig
Miss America — Catherine Wagner

FICTION

Flet: A Novel — Joyelle McSweeney
The Mandarin — Aaron Kunin